Biographies

Frederick Douglass
Voice for Freedom

by Kremena Spengler

Consultant:
Larry E. Hudson Jr., Associate Professor of History
Frederick Douglass Institute for African-American Studies
University of Rochester
Rochester, New York

Capstone press

Mankato, Minnesota

Fact Finders is published by Capstone Press,
151 Good Counsel Drive, P.O. Box 669, Mankato, Minnesota 56002.
www.capstonepress.com

Library of Congress Cataloging-in-Publication Data
Spengler, Kremena.
    Frederick Douglass : voice for freedom / by Kremena Spengler.
    p. cm.—(Fact finders. Biographies)
    Summary: "A brief introduction to the life of Frederick Douglass, the public speaker
and editor who worked to end slavery in the United States"—Provided by publisher.
    Includes bibliographical references and index.
    ISBN-13: 978-0-7368-5434-4 (hardcover)
    ISBN-10: 0-7368-5434-7 (hardcover)
    1. Douglass, Frederick, 1818–1895—Juvenile literature. 2. Abolitionists—United
States—Biography—Juvenile literature. 3. African American abolitionists—Biography
—Juvenile literature. 4. Antislavery movements—United States—Juvenile literature.
I. Title. II. Series.
E449.D75S67 2006
973.8'092—dc22   2005015593

Editorial Credits

Jennifer Besel, editor; Juliette Peters, set designer; Linda Clavel, book designer;
    Kelly Garvin, photo researcher/photo editor

Photo Credits

Corbis/Bettmann, cover, 13, 15 (portrait), 18–19
Courtesy National Park Service, Museum Management Program and Frederick Douglass
    National Historic Site, 8, 20, 25
Getty Images Inc./Hulton Archive, 26; Time Life Pictures, 27
The Granger Collection, New York, 5, 7, 9, 10–11, 15 (newspaper), 16, 17
Howard University Archives/Moorland-Spingarn Research Center, 12
Library of Congress, 1, 21, 22–23, 24

J B
DOUGLASS, F.

C. 1

1 2 3 4 5 6 11 10 09 08 07 06

Table of Contents

Chapter 1

A Speaker Is Born

Frederick Douglass was terrified. He had no idea what he was going to say. He looked at the crowd in front of him. Everyone in the meeting hall strained to see his face. Trembling with nervousness, the runaway **slave** began to speak.

Frederick talked about his life as a slave. He stuttered his first sentences. But he spoke from his heart. As he went on, he became more and more sure of himself. His voice became more powerful.

A wave of excitement passed through the room. When Frederick stepped down from the platform, the crowd broke into wild **applause**.

Frederick was only 23 years old when he joined the fight to end slavery.

William Lloyd Garrison, a famous **abolitionist**, walked up to Frederick. His eyes were full of tears. Like others in the room, he fought against slavery. He asked the crowd if Frederick was property or a man. "A man, a man!" the people shouted.

That night in Nantucket, Massachusetts, Frederick joined the struggle against slavery. He would become one of the best speakers of his time.

Chapter 2

Life in Slavery

Frederick Augustus Washington Bailey was born in Maryland in February 1818. His mother was a slave. So when he was born, Frederick was also a slave. Slaves were not free to live as they wished. They were considered property.

As a young boy, Frederick was happy and safe living with his grandparents. But at age 6, Frederick was old enough to work in the fields. He was forced to leave his cabin home to live with his owner, Aaron Anthony. Anthony treated slaves badly. Slaves who didn't do what he said were beaten.

Sophia Auld taught Frederick that the lines on the page made letters and words.

Learning to Read

When Frederick turned 8, Anthony lent him to Hugh and Sophia Auld in Baltimore, Maryland. Sophia began teaching Frederick to read, but Hugh made her stop. So Frederick worked hard to teach himself to read and write.

It took six years for Frederick to find and save enough money to buy his first book. He bought *The Columbian Orator*. As Frederick read the book, he learned some people thought slaves should be free. He agreed.

New Masters

In 1831, Frederick's life changed again. His owner died and Frederick became the property of Thomas Auld. Auld moved Frederick to St. Michaels, Maryland.

The first book Frederick owned was a popular school book in the 1800s. ▼

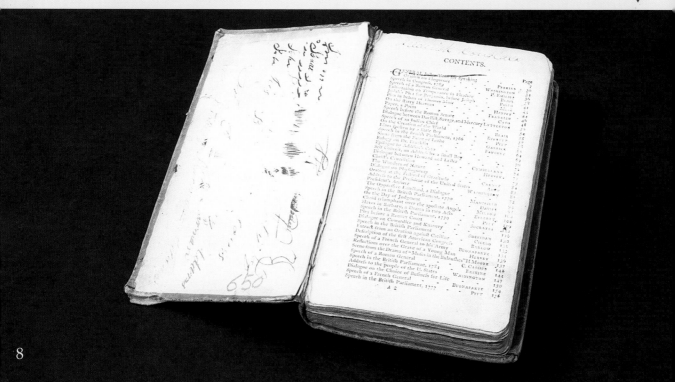

In St. Michaels, Frederick started teaching other slaves to read. Auld did not want slaves to learn. To punish Frederick, Auld sent him to a farmer known for his cruelty to slaves. Frederick was forced to work in the fields day and night. He was **whipped** for not working hard enough.

▲ Slaves had to work many hours tending crops. Frederick worked in fields of wheat and tobacco.

Wishing for Freedom

Frederick wanted to be free. But attempting to escape slavery was very dangerous. If found, slaves would be sent back to their owners or be killed.

In 1836, Frederick planned to escape. But his plan was discovered. Auld's family wanted to sell Frederick. Instead, Auld sent Frederick back to Baltimore to live with Hugh and Sophia.

FACT!

Frederick was taken to jail when his escape plan was discovered. Frederick spent a week in jail while Auld decided if he would sell him to another owner.

Chapter 3

Escape from Slavery

Although his first plan failed, Frederick wanted to be free more than ever. In Baltimore, the 20-year-old met a free black woman named Anna Murray. Frederick wanted to marry her, but slaves could not marry who they wanted.

Another Try

The young man planned another escape. Frederick borrowed a black sailor's traveling papers. Black people had to carry papers that proved they were allowed to travel. Without these papers, even a free black person could be sold back into slavery.

Frederick jumped on a train like this just as it pulled out of the station.

Frederick worried the papers would give him away. The papers had the sailor's name and description. He did not look like the man they described. But dressed as a sailor, Frederick boarded a train going north.

Luckily, the train conductor only glanced at the papers. Frederick was on his way to freedom.

Frederick changed trains and boats several times. After a day of traveling, he arrived in New York. There he was free to start a family and work for himself. Frederick wrote to Anna Murray to join him in New York.

FACT!

At one point during his escape, Frederick met a man he knew. The man started asking questions. Frederick managed to move on before the man could give him away.

Anna Murray gave Frederick all her savings to help him escape. ➤

Out of Slavery

Frederick and his new wife settled in New Bedford, Massachusetts, in 1838. Frederick changed his last name to Douglass, so his master would not find him. Although Frederick had escaped, he was not free by law. If he was found, his master could force him back into slavery.

Even in the North, blacks were not always treated **equally**. Many white people didn't want to work with black people. Frederick had to take jobs no one else wanted to make money for his wife and children.

In New Bedford, Frederick worked many jobs, including a job as a ship builder. ➡

Chapter 4

Freedom

In 1841, friends invited Frederick to an abolitionist meeting in Nantucket. They asked him to tell his story.

Frederick's speech in Nantucket changed his life. Abolitionist leaders heard him. William Lloyd Garrison asked him to join the fight against slavery.

Frederick and Garrison became good friends. Garrison ran a newspaper called *The Liberator*. He printed articles against slavery. Many people read about Frederick's speeches in the newspaper. Together, Frederick and Garrison wrote letters, articles, and speeches to fight for the freedom of all slaves.

William Lloyd Garrison ran *The Liberator* for over 30 years.

Life as a Speaker

In the next several years, Frederick gave hundreds of speeches. He traveled to many states, including New York, Ohio, and Indiana.

Frederick was a powerful speaker. He was smart. He had a strong, deep voice. He could express many feelings, from humor to anger.

Frederick spoke of his experience as a slave. People were moved by his powerful stories. They began to understand how badly slaves were treated.

▲ Frederick, middle left, attended many antislavery meetings.

FACT!

Some people refused to let the abolitionists speak in their buildings. When this happened, the abolitionists gave their speeches outside.

Working as a speaker was difficult and dangerous. Frederick had to travel a lot. Many trains had separate cars for blacks. But Frederick would not sit in these cars. He sat in train cars with his white friends.

Some people did not like the abolitionists' ideas. These people would chase and even beat the speakers. At a meeting in Indiana, an angry mob attacked the speakers. Frederick's right hand was broken.

QUOTE

"If there is no struggle, there is no progress."
—Frederick Douglass

Although it was dangerous, Frederick continued to speak out against slavery. ▼

Chapter 5

An Independent Mind

People could not believe a runaway slave spoke so well. Some people said Frederick must have been born free. To prove his story, he wrote a book about his life in 1845. He called his book *Narrative of the Life of Frederick Douglass.*

Frederick feared the book might lead his master to him. Leaving his family in Massachusetts, Frederick moved to England for safety. He continued to give speeches against slavery.

Two years later, English abolitionists bought Frederick's freedom. They paid Frederick's owner about $700. Frederick no longer had to worry about being forced back into slavery. He was a free man.

NARRATIVE

OF THE

LIFE

OF

FREDERICK DOUGLASS,

AN

AMERICAN SLAVE.

WRITTEN BY HIMSELF.

BOSTON:
PUBLISHED AT THE ANTI-SLAVERY OFFICE,
No. 25 CORNHILL
1845.

Frederick Douglass

Frederick's first autobiography sold 4,500 copies in only three months.

Although he had no formal education, Frederick continued to read and learn throughout his life.

New Ideas

While in England, Frederick's ideas had changed. He had learned how hard it was for slaves in England to gain their freedom. He no longer believed slavery in the United States could be ended peacefully.

When he returned home, Frederick and his family moved to Rochester, New York. There, Frederick was able to form his own ideas on how to end slavery.

Frederick's longtime friend, William Lloyd Garrison, was not pleased. He believed slavery could be ended with nonviolence. Frederick and Garrison's friendship was torn apart.

To share his new ideas, Frederick started his own newspaper, called *The North Star*. In the paper, Frederick wrote articles against slavery. He supported the new **Republican** Party. The party was against slavery. He tried to persuade people to **vote** for Republicans.

Frederick's newspaper got its name because slaves trying to escape at night followed the North Star.

QUOTE

"I recognize the Republican Party as the anchor of the colored man's political hopes and the ark of his safety."
—Frederick Douglass

Chapter 6

The Later Years

In 1860, Republican Abraham Lincoln was elected president. Southern states feared he would end slavery. Several states left the Union. This action led to the Civil War (1861–1865) between the North and the South. Frederick helped blacks sign up to fight in the North's army.

In 1865, the North won the war and the southern states rejoined the union. The government passed the 13th Amendment to the Constitution, freeing all slaves. But freedom from slavery didn't always mean blacks were free to live and work how they wanted. The freed slaves were poor and uneducated. Many white people would not give them jobs. Frederick spoke out. He wanted the government to help blacks.

Black soldiers fought for the North during the Civil War. Frederick helped convince President Lincoln to let blacks fight.

As a U.S. marshal, Frederick was in charge of keeping peace in the community.

QUOTE

"To those who have suffered in slavery I can say, I too have suffered . . . To those who have battled for liberty, brotherhood, and citizenship, I can say, I too have battled . . ."
—Frederick Douglass

Working Hard

Frederick worked very hard even after the slaves were freed. He wrote two more books about his life. These books had more details than his first book. He included the names of his old owners. Frederick also gave speeches throughout the country about equality for blacks and for women.

At the time, few black people had government jobs. But Frederick was very respected. He was appointed marshal for the District of Columbia. He also served as U.S. minister to Haiti.

Still Fighting

Frederick never let the color of his skin stop him. In 1882, Frederick's wife died. Two years later, he married again. But this woman, Helen Pitts, was white.

In the 1800s, many people thought blacks and whites should not marry. They were angry that Frederick married a white woman. Even his family turned against him. But Frederick would not let skin color affect his marriage.

When Helen Pitts married Frederick, her family stopped speaking to her. ▼

Even in his later years, Frederick was well-known for his views on equality.

FACT!

The day he died, Frederick had just returned from giving a speech to support equality for women. He believed women should be allowed to vote, just like men.

The Last Word

Even into his 70s, Frederick was a champion for equal rights. But on February 20, 1895, Frederick spoke his last words. He had just returned home from giving a speech when he suddenly fell to the floor. As his wife knelt beside him, Frederick died of a heart attack.

Frederick Douglass was one of the most powerful speakers of the 1800s. He used his talents to fight for freedom and equality for all people. Today, Americans enjoy the rights Frederick worked so hard to gain.

Fast Facts

Full name: Frederick Augustus Washington Bailey; later changed his last name to Douglass.

Birth: February 1818

Death: February 20, 1895

Hometown: Talbot County, Maryland

Parents: Harriet Bailey; father unknown

Wives: Anna Murray; Helen Pitts

Children: Rosetta, Lewis, Frederick Jr., Charles, Annie

Major achievements:

Started an abolitionist newspaper called *The North Star*

Published three autobiographies

Was a leading voice in the fight against slavery

Time Line

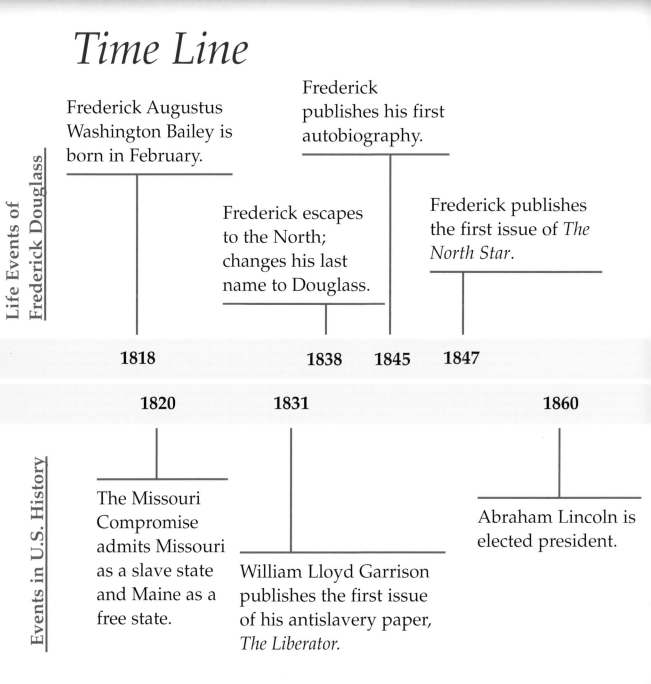

Life Events of Frederick Douglass

Frederick Augustus Washington Bailey is born in February.

Frederick publishes his first autobiography.

Frederick escapes to the North; changes his last name to Douglass.

Frederick publishes the first issue of *The North Star*.

1818   1838   1845   1847

1820   1831   1860

Events in U.S. History

The Missouri Compromise admits Missouri as a slave state and Maine as a free state.

William Lloyd Garrison publishes the first issue of his antislavery paper, *The Liberator*.

Abraham Lincoln is elected president.

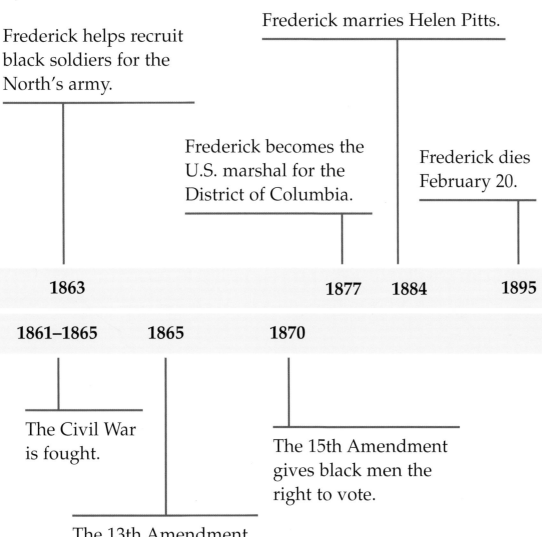

Frederick helps recruit black soldiers for the North's army.

Frederick marries Helen Pitts.

Frederick becomes the U.S. marshal for the District of Columbia.

Frederick dies February 20.

1863   1877   1884   1895

1861–1865   1865   1870

The Civil War is fought.

The 13th Amendment ends slavery.

The 15th Amendment gives black men the right to vote.

Glossary

abolitionist (ab-uh-LISH-uh-nist)—someone who worked to end slavery

applause (uh-PLAWZ)—clapping from a large group

equal (EE-kwuhl)—having the same rights and opportunities as someone else, regardless of race

Republican (ri-PUHB-li-kuhn)—a political party in the United States that believed in ending slavery

slave (SLAYV)—someone who is owned by another person and thought of as property

vote (VOHT)—to make a choice in an election or poll

whip (WIP)—to beat something; slaves were often whipped by their owners.

Internet Sites

FactHound offers a safe, fun way to find Internet sites related to this book. All of the sites on FactHound have been researched by our staff.

Here's how:

1. Visit *www.facthound.com*
2. Type in this special code **0736854347** for age-appropriate sites. Or enter a search word related to this book for a more general search.
3. Click on the **Fetch It** button.

FactHound will fetch the best sites for you!

Read More

Haugen, Brenda. *Frederick Douglass: Slave, Writer, Abolitionist.* Signature Lives. Minneapolis: Compass Point Books, 2005.

Landau, Elaine. *The Abolitionist Movement.* Cornerstones of Freedom. New York: Children's Press, 2004.

Lantier, Patricia. *Frederick Douglass.* Raintree Biographies. Austin, Texas: Raintree Steck-Vaughn, 2003.

Index